ANAHO

ANAHO

STEPHANIE V SEARS

New York

ANAHO
Copyright © 2023 Stephanie V Sears. All Rights Reserved

A special thanks to Expanded Field, The Coe Review, LitBreak, SORTES, Anak Sastra, The Hudson View, Empirical Magazine, Neologism Poetry, The Mystic Blue Review, Culinary Origami, Fleas on the Dog, Adelaide Magazine, Red Ogre Review, Down in the Dirt Magazine, New Reader Magazine NRM, The Headlight Review, and New Contrast Lit Magazine, SA, where some of these poems first appeared.

Cover watercolor by Richard Sears

ARTEIDOLIA PRESS
New York

arteidolia.com/arteidolia-press

First Edition
Library of Congress Control Number: 2023910246
ISBN: 978-1-7369983-9-7

To the one of birch forest and purest rivers

POEMS in ANAHO

Moana*

Savai'i - 1
Little Island - 2
Pacificus - 3
Haven - 4
Palm Tree - 5
Capture Possession Escape - 6
Islander - 8
Basalt Princess - 9
Haka'iki - 10
The Cook of Hatiheu - 12
Pacific Passage - 14
One Afternoon at Teahupo - 15
Nights of Raivavae - 16
Laurent - 18
Other Others, or a B2 Stealth Bomber - 19
A Cargo Lounge Heroine - 20
Buccaneer Bliss - 21
Dying a Motorcyclist - 22
Toi et Moi - 23
Third Visit - 24
Teleported - 25
Evidence - 26
Anaho - 27

*Lagoon

Bokeh*

The Duke of Pastrana - 31
When My Back is Turned - 32
Leap - 33
Out of the Woods - 34
Set Back From the Road - 35
Looking Through the Trees - 36
Tintagel - 37
Not Nearly Enough Forest - 38
Portrait of a Lute - 40
Red Mood - 41

Encounter in Dorsoduro – 42
Beginning of a Passion – 43
Sottoportego – 44
Cupola – 45
Return – 46
Letters – 47
Siberian Solace – 48
Seduction – 49
Breeze Through a Cherry Tree – 50
Man from Iceland – 52
Short-lived Hospitality – 53
Le Gisant – 54
Leaf-Sweeper – 55
Mistakes – 56
Bitter Taste – 58
Puma Weather – 59
Stampede – 60
Night Fauna – 61
Stalking a Dialogue – 62
Moon Fox – 64
November, Four pm – 65
A Japanese Garden in a French Mind – 66
The Capital – 67

*Japanese term for a blurred luminous background in photography

Phantoms

Sissi's Villa – 71
Red Gloves in Umbria – 72
Transformation – 74
Pisani Palace – 76
Alter Ego – 77
The Last Morning – 78
On the Moon – 79
Hunedoara – 80
A Case for Reincarnation – 82
Chemistry – 83
Light Stepping – 84
Himalayan Foothills – 85
What Snuck up on Them – 86
In the Silence After the Bird's Call – 88
A Kind of Anniversary – 89
Paradise Predicted – 90

MOANA

Savai'i

The ocean
we rush to it
with polished bodies, in fresh bathing, despair.
In our blue sense of space
we dart like fish
beneath lucent waves,
above fluid floors
braced against basalt walls and powdery strands.
Loving with fragrant digits –
humid buds sundered from tropical loam –
we sit dark-limbed in yawning caves,
happy but listless infants under a spell,
in ceaseless bliss, wishing to drown.

Little Island

Evening reclines around the bay's
pellucid plait of reef and silence,
strewing blossoms on the sand,
pink feelers darted red,
collecting the inconstant dole of dreams
lured from the alluviums of the mind,
honoring all of them utterly.

The sunset sheds gold and red
west of a sister isle.
On this side, palms quiver,
coal black
against the vast wager of the sea.

Flop, rush. Rolling out bantam tides,
parrotfish, black-tip sharks, bonito
tune their scales, thread silver and rainbow
into the night set with moon and stars
whose godly imprints
intangibly prevail.

Pacificus

Trees disheveled and lank,
their foliage sings and scuttles
in animal ways.
Nuts drop
with blunt wisdom,
appointing leisure to the day.
The ocean steadies the cadence,
driving over coral
what once was lost
or promised.
The sky cruises along,
puffing cheroots.
At disputed boundaries
do palms lean on the stars,
are stars upheld by fronds?
Is it wake or trance?

Haven

We were summoned by pelagic mystery
through a thousand fronds
blown through by trade winds.
Cutting greens and blues like a prow,
the room had myriad suns and shadows,
gold, dark wood, pantheons, disciples,
the perfumed prowess of heaven.

Palm Tree

The horizon's lungs fill with light
for islanders to live carefree.

Ocean rolls into sky
seeding pink robin dawns

and solar dusters,
alkalescent between swell and star.

A nut's porcelain falls
to sapphire soliloquies,

to the black marble of dorsal fins,
soil's salt and shell.

Dream swash-buckles here and there,
then turns the tiller

towards tousled isles
registered in Eden's log.

In soporific bays, like children,
coconuts roll about in sand,

until solitude touches their palms
with the hurt of an expanding sky.

Capture   Possession   Escape

Capture
    Farthest reach of farthest island.
    Savannah pitched by
    salt   wind   wild.
    Horses smelted from basalt
    exhaled by mist.
    For the soul's ecology
    ocean mirroring sky's glower.
    Midday draws the recumbent line of *Fiu**
    even though stars know the way
    to this demiurgic land.

    The swift exactitude of riders
    captures sunlight
    when they gallop in a sheen of muscle.
    Then night gathers them
    around her like campfires
    before fears of sorcery bewitch them.

Possession
    Alone in the swank of silence
    on the great highland above the sea
    where none live.
    Satrap to that province
    between her blood and soul.
    Through fog's raiment she walks
    beside her body.
    Chaste in a spring pool by the trail
    as before and after the birth of being.
    Planets whisper and pull.
    Under the fairy terns' wafting
    she staggers into nostalgia
    unable to rescue the instant
    when the glittering sea and
    cliff-sprung trees
    beset by spirits
    part for a view of Neverland.

Escape
    Her feet touch the cargo deck
    pentacle of escape
    quiet in a black brimstone bay
    where time reaffirms itself.
    The ship greets her errant ways
    absconding her
    while those left ashore
    fade back
    into a banyan's abiding shade.

Fiu: boredom, melancholy

Islander

Big and skillful,
eyes sliced slim and
sidelong on his face
made words go numb.

The simmer of violence, if any,
nature disciplined.

His island was predisposed to silence
through the lone hoot of the *Karavia*.
We both drew on that quiet
like sailors on halyards,
feeling our hearts' hemp
twist and tighten.

Once apart, we called out
over the unselfconscious miles,
returning language
to its numinous form.

We summoned each other
across star-distilling hills,
lunar bolts of sea.

It even happened that, overcome
by distance, we carved initials
in the pulp of trees.

Basalt Princess

Pacific lunges for the valley.
In stares   see-throughs,
in fuchsia dawns and hell fire dusks.
With a latent thrust of impudence,
outer space beckons to the sea trench.

This once was her isle –
with its quenching guava scrub,
manioc, taro fields, mango orchards,
decorous breadfruit trees –
glugging the sky
between Capricorn and Equator.

She opens the shadows of her house to me.
Looks me up and down until
I ebb into remoteness.
Ninety years have streamlined
her down to timelessness.

Crowned with island rose and
porpoise teeth weaving buds
with their mortuary ivory.
Glory still nestles in the furrows
of her face smoked in tattoos,
a Brueghel blue of soot and thunder
from head to toe.

Her voice, a blast of surf,
a dark inclusion in a storm's crystal.
I can see her as then,
draped in royal *tapa*,*
one splendid smooth arm
fanning the drowsy air.

Then my own time topples
when, suddenly clairvoyant,
she predicts that money
will devastate the world.

Tapa: white mulberry bark cloth

*Haka'iki**

Large looms this figure of a man,
anonymous in yellow waterproof,
though, about him,
crowned and sceptered,
a stark quiet commands.

From Ua Pou to Hiva Oa
we are too many on board.
Each swell amplifies
signs of bad luck.

In night's bucking brine
and onrushing space
the boat shackles me
to windlass and capstan.
I reach for the sky's cosmic wallpaper,
kite heart cannoned upward
on a string of destiny.
Knees and feet grow wings
over the next soaring crag,
casting a pall over the stars.

He stands as barbican
against the livid depths
fathoms down in my imagining
their indifferent swallow.

Even as exhaustion seizes mind and flesh,
prepares them for drowning,
a thread of rebellion
weaves through me,

seesawing off the shoals. Safety
was never part of this scheme.
He makes that clear
with battlefield arms
lathered in salt and tattoos.

Holds me inside the thick brackets
of his muscles, corrugated chest
warding off waves, wind, and fate.

Thaumaturge to his people,
king to their yearnings,
he cradles me in his lineage
of harbors and valleys.

Until I fall asleep, his copper face
awash with my hair.

* *Haka'iki*: chief, king

The Cook of Hatiheu

Koute was mistress   to high peaks

prattling slopes   skulls   anointed bones.

Basalt cuspids bit hard into the obsidian sea
while the valley ate from her hand.

On Sundays
                    roaring waves appeased
by church chimes

slumbered emeraldine
along a dream-fracking beach.

Bare-foot valley rife with souls
was all shudder and shimmer.
Here   *Koute*   mother

to the Humboldt current

lifted sea-hounds on the hunt
of wahoo and skipjack.

Night's thalassic embrace
nourished air and soil.
Under its cosmic ardor she cooked
                    the way others write music

between roof and stars   an open hearth
licking flames from her eyes

as she fed them rainbow and cirrus foods.

Chevrettes flour-rolled into asteroids.
Breadfruit manna
                    sea-salt sanded.
Pink florets of frigate tuna
                    coated in lime and milk.

Night's sagoma was close enough to feel
so that *Koute* served us distance too
                              tiare buds of space
celestial jellies   supersonic eels

The rule of the dark was prodigy.

Tirelessly young
            we sat up till dawn's collation.
Her clansmen emerged then
                        from translucence
                leaving a bracken fragrance
and mangos at my door.

Pacific Passage

Night ocean aches with moonlight
and sharks switchblade the shadow
from constellation to constellation.
Ambling through a vapor of stars,
ship unravels spools of space,
even as it tows a longing.
Yet ship eventually forgets itself
in the capsized conceit
of omniscience.

I am in the habit of these cosmic passages,
sweet on open sky insomnia,
alongside the fugitive seamanship of cockroaches.
A godmother dream occasionally blesses me,
plying my orbital sleep with planets.

Instead of rooster, captain crows:
'*Amai**, we'll be first to see this dawn.'
Five am flakes our faces with gold
at the fringe of a genesis where neither
revelation nor enigma require choosing.

From Rapa to Tubuai, horizon exceeds itself.
Building fire and sanguineous manors
in the grave act of silence, greeting us
in firmament's carmine and magenta entrails.
All around us, inspirations take shape,
slow-moving, grand with peplum splendor.
Quiet is the creation of the pelagic sea.
Night's half-truths were less forceful
and now we are precisely folded
in the origami of a master player.

**Amai*: come

One Afternoon at Teahupo

Tropics' billboard veranda
As flimsy as a good wish card,
Happy with the blue and green makeup
Painting its windows and balustrade.
Small house plays peacock.
Grating planks underfoot
Hover between un-planed timber and home.
View out-leagues the rustic cottage
With light shafts and marine scintillations.
Sun lords over square miles of ocean.
A flock of bobbing surfers,
Dressed in bare sinew,
Use the wing of their backs,
Keen to undulation and slide,
Targeting two realms.
Here and now propagates
Through the sharp intake of breath.
Off the horizon a gloss of silence.
I, honed by fragrance and flux
Of vanilla and brine, am seen
By the skyline's fish eye.
I free a catharsis of syllables
To formulate tranquility
Of the endless phrase
In a monochrome of gold
At this time
Surfers rewound by a constant cameraman.
Sun steam meets sun shower
Cutting facets on weather's gem.

A pink balloon caught in a tree
Turns itself into a barrel-man.

Nights of Raivavae

They chant nights
into perpetuity
war-like or tender orchestrations
funneled through *a capella*

Odysseys and improvising skies
taught them to sing so
in absolutes
to foil lacerating departures
and for alakazams of return

Bequeathed open sea
they surf like-minded
on the fretwork of bastion waves
on star-woven winds

The reef fires
pelagic cylinders
sparks yards of pyretic hair
in the night's amnion

Flames chip at monolithic features

Outsider appended to the rituals
by childish infatuation
Siblings strap to my neck
to the pontoon of my legs

Smell of whelps on my skin
from a spell of possession
I sift tales from coral sand
brother sister spiraling into shells

How we succumb to each other
the euphonious islanders and I
in a contract unsigned

They situate me in intervals
between peak and cloud
cultivate me to favor
their broad-leaf crops
Pride churns between us
invents new tribalisms

Nothing can ever beat the moon's
sweep through the trees
or the bacterial lucency
in the lagoon's sapphire eye

The heart of Raivavae night
vanquished calamity

Laurent

Of that cool blaze
between trident and chariot,
beyond the frayed edges of purpose
and the inflexible timing of beauty,

red boy with shoal green eyes
is forever the maker and master.

Sun freckled, salamander slim,
woodsy beneath the *Mape* trees,
chiseled by island solitude,

begotten by a Polish girl in need of time
a Frenchman failed to give her,

lost to them because elsewhere
in the mind of a dreamer
unburdened by the procession of years.

Converted by ecclesiastical ferns,
baptized in leaf fountains,

with his child's limbs taking to
the black armored peaks that
fasten orchids to combed falls,

amphibian at sunset
when fish hop like hares,

at night sizing stellar carats,
strung between sand-rooted trees,
spellbound by the fey likeness of himself.

Other Others, or a B2 Stealth Bomber

After dinner star gazers
picket the jetty
with fishing rods,
casting and reeling in
ocean's bullion.

Their angler rites utter
a full moon prayer,
adjusting infinity
to their cosmic corner.

Long ago, the island was
allotted immensity and,
perchance, visits from elsewhere.

Then space came near
and the whole land
capsized into mythology:

a pneumatic beast
with a cyclopean eye,
tantalum sheen,
performed its dressage:
forward, stop, backward, left.

Glowered, hummed, until nothing
of insular pride remained
but coral dust on an alien's chart.

A Cargo Lounge Heroine

The small tonnage cargo
privy to south pacific moods,
was obligated to swell and wind
for its fearless disposition.
High up on the castle
a wide-eyed lounge tilting
to sea and sky
offered the unyielding rover
a tern's weightless pause.

In dawn's watered inks
land couldn't keep me.
I was picked off islands
heavy with lithic spells and iron trees
by a big-armed crew.
They held me up to the restive air
by my wing tips.
If a leeward cuff of breeze still fettered me
to sandy shallows,
adventure soon intruded.

At my wayward elbow, a wood bar
polished like an English Major
stuck in an outpost,
metallized with the brogue of tankards
and cocktail utensils,
concocted me a homecoming
from the *soon, not yet,* a distant *perhaps.*

When a shark hide sailor
turned Beethoven on loud
for the dolphins combing the prow,
a green island wrung from the horizon,
became elixir of joy.

I went scouting ahead of myself
to make sure we'd never arrive.

Buccaneer Bliss

I cannot but liken the hard lines of your chest
to the muscular crush of the reef,
as it keeps back the bass world
– that modulates such ponderous operas of grief –
and spends its long-traveled vigor
on unstrained shores where crustaceans sashay.
What might have been lost under time's rubble,
its one chance penned in diary notes,
lolls on its own falcate beach, for volcanic idols
collecting plump blooms and full-bellied fruit
that hang low to be munched in tribute.
Jell-O nights wobble and stretch as if barely born,
and like you, every palm rests its untidy head
against the coolness of a star.
I can but liken some noble part of you
to that basalt assaulted by foam.
Mercurial dawn finds you perched, osprey
aligning wings to the trade wind
over shoal depths, mere metaphors
of a buccaneer bliss once rehearsed,
now glittering blue.

Dying a Motorcyclist

You had already died
by the time we met,
dense already like granite,
a statue shimmering in a froth of leaves.
Unable to reach beyond youth
– I guessed it –
an epic carving
profiled in the bronze cladding
of a palatial staircase,   even though
you still lived in the wildest places,
pared down
to few words,
to the reverberating sadness
that was your singular charm.
You wore campfire clothes,
color of thatch and mud,
crannied with pockets.
In the *mordoré* eyes:
gilded raptors,
a feathering of fronds
induced by warm seas, and
a last rush of enticement.
After which your tires traced a Z
in the mud, and off the caldera's cliff,
into the waterfall, you crashed.

Toi et Moi

The formula abides near silver-leafed streams,
sculpting the slumber of poreless rock,
soaking plots of *papa moko* fern.
Here our differences shrink, we submit
to the coastline's sparkle
when the ocean shimmers under the moon
and sun, and stone exhales its furnace smell.
Your kind of silence conquers the night,
your chest is bound in stars,
waves and comets curl and shoot through your hair,
your patience wears its silk pennants,
your arms are equinox tides.
You fastened 'your way' on like armor.
We swear only by spirits
hauled in by the tentacles
of the octopus tree we sit under.
Because of you, I too, am well beyond wild.

Third Visit

You and I skip along,
sweet-fleshed with leaf sap and tide,
feet chirping in the sand,
careful that each print
indelibly marks our place
on this beach of white flour and petals –
free of tyranny
struggles and shame.

Intuition grants us a scent of rapture.
As it should be.

Hoohoo… sings a bird,
letting silence prevail,
hoohoo in the green bank of trees,
grown thicker and darker,
when the sun placed its chin on the sea.
Nature's way redeems us.

Across the sable night
blue crabs write epigraphs.
It rains a shower of blossoms,
whose perfunctory death offsets
the birth of tomorrow's new batch.

Constant replication ensures our return.

Teleported

On the windblown rind of Easter Island,
I ride a lean pony named Flaco,
even as I ride the metro
from Alma to Filles du Calvaire.
The tunnel's coal stench,
the train's borborygmus,
revisit rocks of salt and lava.
Far below, the pelagic blue
tows my horse's greed
for cliff-growing dandelions.
Rongorongo, all ours,
barely keeps out
an ocean tasseled
with frigate wings.
I sit by my horse, holding
the rope reins against his fall.
A stout sky, sheared
by screeching and moon's
pale scythe,
makes me miss my stop.

Evidence

I have walked into these dendroid grimoire greens
of Ambarella, Mape and Banyan,
turning my back on the ocean's barricade,
towards the inhuman core
of these twenty one kilometers
drawing the Pacific's loneliest oval.
The forest pulse has fastened onto my heart beat,
keeping pace with exploration's solitude.
I see no end to this woodland
growing dark ahead of me,
psyche's perpetual grove.
Archangel ferns flutter wings at my knees.
Seeded here by chance,
their exhalations articulate
a savage idiom of silence
which initiates me
to universal antipodes.
At low tide the island expands,
drawing new ground plans
on the lagoon's painted halo.
Inland, it reveals polysemous spaces,
feigned by myth and parable.
Aberrant spirits contort and crystallize,
to will my attention
on troglomorphic shapes
disentangling from moss and fiber.
Slow creatures, they pretend a statue's stillness.
At a second glance, caught in the act
of unclear intentions.
The coast was the edge of a well,
at the bottom of which I fell
on a rash of impatiens flowers.
Insane with isolation, they proliferate
and terrorize.

Anaho

Forever is mid-morning in Anaho Bay.
No moonlight, storm, or sunset will inflict
their vengeful melancholy on us.

Mid-morning displays a surveyor's accurate arc
and a sequence of turquoise, gold and green,
row by row as in a rainbow.

Vast and uniformed father,
the sky plays only a distant role.

Anaho, whiz illustrator to all south sea tales,
obliterates the torrid bug-bitten brush
I came through.

A thousand emblems diffuse their variations on love.
I must remain still, like a pontiff deep in prayer
or I'll shatter in as many shards.

Silence plays the music of palpitation, undulation.

Shallow sea trespasses on the sand
with an amphibian's hunch for another way of life.
Casuarina and palm lean toward water with castaway thirst.

A man washes his horse in the bay,
showing muscle, though he never self-reflects
as I do. I will not call out, he will not wave,

the horse will stand beside him,
the breeze always mollifying,
the sea hardly rippling.

The three of us repeat ourselves,
eternalize the instant,
save each other from interruption.

Only the fringing reef battles its way
towards the indigo opening
of the enfolding bay.

BOKEH

The Duke of Pastrana

What anachronism
binds yesterday night's agitation
to a portrait exposed among the Prado Velasquez'?

I remember you
Don Gregorio de Silva Mendoza y Sandoval,
as you stand
accoutered in history,
in the Cimmerian distance of the canvas.
I recognize the fall of black hair
down your back, it could be mine to breathe,
its aroma trickled through my thoughts,
as I walked today
through Madrid's dun streets
where lustrous horses swayed like flags
to a march.

I've known other warriors
— Rajput, Maori —
to hold the riddle of their age and strength
in the expansive sweep of their hair.
Though they never touched me,
they always found me
on some stretch of premonition.

Duke of Pastrana,
are you not that Spaniard,
with hound, horse and rapier,
sailing across two oceans
to a warm island dreamt of gold?
Am I not its harbor
shot through by lightning,
the blue waters off its conquered coast?

When My Back is Turned

Did we just enter 'The Invention of Morel'
and lose our way in
Halong Bay, imprisoned
between cabochon archipelagos,
as in memory's tricked circuit?
An ever rehearsed encounter,
trailed by Vietnamese girls
calling out to you:
"You there, beautiful brute,"
while we verged on a vow never made.

Leap

Drenched in rain's evergreen,
the terrace simulates a teak pond.

A sill Sssing along a cliff,
– the vertical incubator of flight and trill –
implores its pardon.

Outside peeks inside,
gets only a mild rebuff.

Birds fan crimson blooms and
lilies broadcast a future to the stars.

Yearning ventilates the brink of the deck,
prey to quake and landslide.

Yet the cliff holds the gaze
in suspense,
in a rose steam hazing
the sky with a sadness
of beauty unhailed

by eyes that hasten by
that hint of death.
A leap of grace
precisely timed, every day,
when the senses slim to spirit.

Up there in expanding silence,
plants oscillate between botany and biology.

Creatures unquote themselves
and disappear,
seek no other formula
than their reticence.

The cliff itself dissipates,
validates an illusion that
gathers, distills, bewitches
right then.

Out of the Woods

The tree line is in green slow-motion,
same as those boreal eyes
that oversee the turpentine forest,
lined afar with fur and howls,
sweeping north to the pole.

A swelling *aria* across my wood front
I heard it… just where he is far.
A rending of nature's even gesture.
A strategic muteness of fallen trunks
arranged in crosses….in rafts of safeguard.
The heart's zeal moves towards some type of faith
between moon, moss, a rampage of hints.

Those rocky, rolling syllables
in his northern toffee voice,
a fluxing mutter between silences
that unfolds love like a napkin.

Now a fire ignites among my brooding trees.
Their council radars between us. Outreaching.
Emotion's leaching up and down the field,
searches for an outlet.

I must try to get to him…

as if in nature's school,
only pines apart, in the smell
of plumbago point pencils
and book pages glazed with bear fat.

The burn of an alliance
at the tree front….
Only this: believing in each other.

Set Back From the Road

Houses singled out by regret and hope,
stand back from the humdrum roads
as milestones of providence.

A cedar grove leans into sun-eyed panes,
looking in like a pack of wolves,
fragrant with an evergreen's howl.

The balustrade around a terraced roof
unties the moorings of a ship,
tracing a wake of seagulls in the sky.

On rainy days a garden drinks its full,
self-absorbed, misty heart
losing itself in private epics.

A front lawn dreams of being
grazed by a herd of sheep,
between party rhododendrons.

At the rear of a house, another view
basted with late sun, by night
constellated with lamplight,

extends into a woodland riddle,
orbits, with bay windows and idleness,
the inner planet of a musing brain.

Looking Through the Trees

Winter transforms sunset into revelation,
Slyly turns a key, releasing
An exclamation into afternoon,
Something from beyond my view.
The illuminated trees brighten into seers
With clever eyes that bore into
What I cannot see. They have begun
To stretch upward,
All the while staying put.
Drawing attention to the sky,
Pulling it in
Like a blue ship,
Sailing it with their branches.
Emancipated by the moment
Into boundless clarity,
The pines chin themselves
Up from pending dusk
Into unstinting space.
Ascending beyond the birds
Until they falter and darken.
The sun paints a last portrait
Which the all-seeing owl signs
With an unflappable swoop,
From limb to limb,
Leaving his nocturnal omen.

Tintagel

From what is left of it, the ocean
extolls a chant of wind and wave,
a woof and crash of bygones.
The colossal profile of legend,
what knows little of time,
extends beyond land's amnesia,
casting off on tides
of emerald sorcery. Returned
by the lithe ritual of dawn,
or done up in carnival sunsets,
it cares little for inland streets
that claim and flaunt it
in a display of quaintness:
stone grimed with moss,
bedded in flowers,
open doorways, eager like salesmen.
The land's vital innards,
held in a cave,
recoil from speculation.
Feeling its bare ribs,
Tintagel goes a step further to sea,
and may simply depart
and history lose a page.

Not Nearly Enough Forest

In the forest of purest things….

Inspiration's endless progeny.
Poetry's long hair dangles,
swirls, dizzy from a stream's
incumbent freedom.

Inventions for which no premise
was ever recorded or filed.
Exergonic.
Given an equal chance at
dismissal or reverence.

An apogee of light radiates
a gnosis through birches,
performs a thousand hand dance
around basking oak trees.

Under the steep tenor of altitude,
a brook multiplies movements
of un-lauded perfection.

Predation, like love,
rewards exertion with sleep,
limp on a branch.

Not nearly enough forest
keeps body from spirit here.
They infuriate each other,

they exchange unrealizable
suggestions of place and emotion
almost possessed.

While under a plain's open sky,
cluttered like an attic
with human archetypes,
another can't even hide
behind thought's stealth.

And when at last collared
by metrics of conformity,
he dissolves into apologies.

Portrait of a Lute

The lute lies mute,
flat on the sound board,
blond like a Circassian bard,
for-playing mesmeric tunes.

Cherry ribs expectant,
tense with music,
like other clever objects
of suspended energy
that share with me
their occult predilection.

Forest skin, veneered
by virions of legend and chivalry,
rustles like sycamore leaves.
Sylvan auras waver
around the peg box
in a ganging of jade,
emerald, tanzanite.

In the crook of a diamond pane
window, a downpour annotates
the parchment of a score
for a *Passacaille* dance,

sheltered from the park's
heroic greens that
outrun the October gale
holding on to full skirts.

A rebel lock of hair
excites a shimmer
down the courses.
The openwork rose
has an elfin face
with mutant eyes
and the nimble stance
of a musical dandy,
moved by every stir.

Red Mood

Walls skinned down to the brick,
sit on their reflections,
calling out through the fog.

Depths of red bleed at ogee-arched windows,
half-naked trees recede into beatific
gardens, beyond all reason.

Bound in desire, the city
is a long kiss offered at every instant.
By the curdled-glass lanterns, it careens

and exhales a pearly mist,
a pining verse written
on its suspended vapors.

Casanova pads towards me.
Collar raised to the structured chin,
his smile stirs a blush in the air.
But as he turns the corner,
in his former place,
dashes by a stray cat.

Encounter in Dorsoduro

Unblemished morning of good luck.
Adriatic sun diligently threads gold
into the algae-ridden steps
varnished with shallow water.
The gothic windows have dressed up
to mystify and inveigle.

Today walks Giorgione's best work.
Here he comes in boldness
nearly flawless
in the gilded zenith of the city's frame.

We scavenge what we can
of the emphatic instant,
side glancing like horses.
I pass as oracle.
He gives me a line.

Wonder shudders in our wake,
even once out of sight.
Better not pursue this further
but store the instant in
the city's immortal files.

Beginning of a Passion

Suddenness, you didn't know yourself
to possess such reserves of intuition,
well before the question of what's next.

An euphonic gasp of minor chords
assails me. From the heart's crystal,
splinters stab the brain,
free of thought's darning:

a delirium of color as from a chorus
of birds, sleeking their orisons
in cavernous trees.

Before this, I was lightening rod
to adolescent premonition
that your land called me,
inventing some stroke of memory.

In spectrums of silence,
I found lucidity, that lone wolf
of streets and meadows.

In someone's sun-ignited hair,
where fir trees trade with wind,
and symbolism solves the enigma.

You. The distant hammering of hooves
of a red horse on the run,
a warlock's jade eye glinting
under winter's strands of fog,

you, twilight's eternal hunt,
the ultimate rescue from drowning,
the dew after the storm.

Moments ever turn the corner,
so that you may reappear.

Sottoportego

Wood-beamed, murky like a galleon's hold,
an echoing passageway overlooked
by a clairvoyant window, though
time's cataract palled the crown glass panes.

A tunnel compressed into a riddle
of a city rafting on audacity,
as I see it from Murano's afar,
under February's cold evening fire,
outlining soaring bell towers.

I want all your secrets.

The window, cornered in Rembrandt fawn,
melted to gold by an inner sun,
seems tangled in unsaid.
Impossible to decrypt its secret toil.
Industrious brick flesh
next to porphyry skin, slowly
battle oils of temptation:
both frame an incarceration
and achieve a still life.
Transfixed by such forever,
I nearly reach the city's core.

Perceivable, a memory
of revel and madness,
of worship and lust,
gashes the senses.

So take me.

Cupola

Clouds strain outside like rowboats
against a winter's cobalt.
Inside, the church swells into another outside,
just out of reach.
Cupola, incubator of heavens,
by way of arched windows above,
rejoices in sunlight.
In the circle's epicenter,
a soft flutter of wings,
magnetized by the rays.
An angelic uplifting of space
snubs gravity.
Unusual geometries cast off
from some drawing board.
Disembodied vision conjures flight,
though the body still hesitates below.
When dusk's bruise appears,
the eyes lose their way again.

Return

In March, month of initiation,
the city is most potent.
A grey wind between Alp and sea
rips at the heart,
paints a glycerin mask
over the bubbled, bandy panes
and their introspective stare.
Bundles of pledges
hunker in corners,
waiting for a star's spell.
The tarnished sun, outlined
by the climatic compass
in the coal-packed sky,
leaves a gold treacle
on seraphs atop churches,
while beyond shadowy walls,
the blond marsh grass
summons an afternoon frost,
a cold wild expansion,
as if on the Volga banks.
Soon, the flat mud planes
glisten, freshly lacquered,
then bevel into a vessel
that departs from the unguarded shore.
Ideas swim, moods ring.
Sounds, soft as feather,
steel-like crimsons,
luscious nude marble,
ruins where dwell ecstasies,
in March's devilment.
In this brilliant waste of transformation
one struggles to keep up.
Tourists meander restlessly,
nagged by transgressions,
and think to die on the spot
so that nothing less
might bewitch them.

Letters

Blue blood of the paper.
Slim martial wounds
by distress once incurred.
The remedy was found
in those caked packets of letters:
mountain of contemplation
as was for Huang Pin-Hung
the stroke of sunlight on a bloom
in those heights near Ch'ing Ch'eng.
Her letters catch me by the sleeve,
even with lines unread,
no longer meaning,
by way of the script,
but as eternal hieroglyphs,
as talismans kept,
as hilltops on a cerulean horizon,
as a summer waterfall,
as an eagle's geometry,
of following invisible parallels.
B, a boat with full sails.
I am the exile of knowing you
to be that wave at the prow.
S snakes through the ash
of our misunderstandings.
Loving you so much,
it was hard to love you well.
Even my betrayals rang false.
C, jungle beauty,
emerald mines of your eyes.
T, gold tug in your heart,
youth of your torment,
nerves of hand to hair.
This crisp mountain of paper
to contemplate,
like Huang Pin-Hung
knowing the rock cliff at dawn,
the flute taste of Spring,
pity's scattered blossoms.

Siberian Solace

Gelid country runs beside the train,
as if I had left the best behind,
tossing at me sheaves of silver birch,
ice shattered into liquid sparkles,
a gold mash of prairie and duck wings.

Let me step out of speed,
far between two oceans,
crowned with tender branches
stripped across the sky,
clotted cromlechs, grass-spiked at my feet
in renewed vows of wilderness.

Exalted sadness belies the happiness,
the chimes of it close and far,
in some resolute marvel of being.
The hearts of those I know,
out-live distance as I stand
in the bright hiatus where
space and earth converse in endless rhyme.

The crows have hidden every fragment of solitude
beneath their blue black quills.
I rely on their perched friendship,
all night, glowing like a worm
under the blinking stars,
exultant, speechless.

Seduction

The cat man is loose in slumber,
stretched between love and predation,
indolent harp ligaments tied to
muscles of lightening and rain,
skin latticed with slyness.

He caressed, struck, unknotting his body
the while, unhinging delight.

Late morning opens lilies.
The sanctuary smell of wood refutes mischief,
though, from half-opened eyes, leaks
the green lime of peril, the decree that
one of us must go.

Breeze Through a Cherry Tree

I

Night went through her
molten and furthering

to a starlight hum
concealing her

in a shimmer of grey threading
belted lilac

arrowed movements
into sheer stillness

unlocking her
from silk shackled hours

of footsteps like kisses
with decorum's cursive hands

magnolia combed hair
now tightly skulled

with no other limbs than
that swaying nimble air

Zigzagging sleuth
determined and occulted

II

The assault leaps out
from a shiver of silence

She twists key sinews
shatters bones opening

a breach to organs that
stiffen already like a winter coat

outspeeds his heart
stems blood flow causing an ebb

bores out the eyes
bursts all the seams

of him longing for her
meekness even as she murders him

she of the rice-powdered nape
of the coy shielded smile

he knew once docile in his bed
Katsumi: Victorious Beauty

Man from Iceland

There was a man from Iceland,
believed to be colder than winter.
Under the pale eve of his brows,
his eyes bore into me
with sea cave fluorescence.

His lips were shaped to hunger,
to seethe and devour
behind their polar front.

In the tapered light of frosted nights,
his cheekbones poked through
the skin as broken wings.

By day, he was the glacier
that concealed his paradox.
Ignited from within,
he poured out humors of ice.

Olympian, he ran
– some said to meet with gods –
in evergreen woods as straight as icicles,
only shadowed by aurora and wind.

In no way cold, but fueled
by immeasurable temperatures
from unfathomed depths.
Erupting volcano.

Short-Lived Hospitality

The well-appointed crypt spared no room
for spirit to roam,
so the buried could play
their elegant back and forth
of residence and absence.

Perfume vials, Mugwort and Rosemary unguents,
trinkets, familiars, sticky with emotion's residues,
were still much enjoyed
in the long shadow of centuries.

A pious gush of maggots
erased their struggles and regrets,
and all their praying through life's ferocities.

A carved arch reverently frames an opening
as if the one supine there needed air,
showering sequins on her
from the wide desert sky.

Millenniums have reordered her space.
A different comfort neatly folds silence,
like organdy in silk paper,
radiates light with crystal bombast.

For just a while, the tomb
transports the visitor
over a stream of skulls,
the callow rift of time,

until a ceiling fresco
gives a taste of paradise.
Jealous of the dead, unwelcome,
he is forced to depart.

Le Gisant

There he lies recumbent
in the champagne summer light,

ferment of clear Calvinist windows
and of a church's stark yard outside,

that sends up an abstinent desert glare
to the carefree sky.

His flaxen sandstone hair undulates,
washed by streams of sunshine.

His Visigoth name has faded
into chronology's forgotten archives.

As once he rode a horse, now he roams
beyond time's pendulum.

Under a barrel vaulting, he breathes
to the mystery of particles and frequencies.

Crowds perceive an awakening
and seek the elixir of his arrant blood

so their senses will at last forget
their own dying.

They press around like children,
humble, though eager for fiercer life,

hands fluttering there to rouse
the kinship that offers relief.

The force of that hope
brings him back!

Leaf Sweeper

Surrender to your helpless life,
bled by each sweep of broom,
on the sidewalk glutted
with the deciduous downpour
of the shade-lush trees,
towards the gutter's chasm,
wiping the constant sweat
off your face.

A broad-shouldered heat
of roasted welkins,
in blues and browns,
over the Chocolate Hills,
makes you breathe hard,
bullies you, my dear fellow,
into a rote of solitude,
as if no one had noticed you,

nor the ghostlings of bliss
that uplift your heart,
even as buses, grimed with sightseers,
pass you with gastric noises.

I am your panoramic view
of the sultry plain
bubbled with hillocks, rocked
by the sea's indigo pendulum.
I know that your humility
is nothing less
than a tiger's pride
in his lonely survival,
without roar or blink,
sweeping your path clean
towards reincarnation.

Mistakes

Horizon extends a hand,
offering cloud blots
as ghostly redoubts.

Spirit draws symbols
in the permissive sky.
Flat yonder levels with reason.
At night, stars absolve all,
in a covenant with instinct.

The red scratch of the Trans-Pantanal
was engineered to capture immensity.
Animalia mistakes the soft highway
for a lounge. Tenderness clings
to harshness as they wallow.
At times they stumble onto
the road's fatal prophecy.

The stag hangs antlers on the sunset.
Macaws fly by as scarves.
A dead anteater hides
behind his feathered tail.
Aqueous and frozen, a caiman
aims a citrine eye
at the careless old fellow,
curled in slumber, or moribund,
beside his sole friend,
an arthritic bicycle.
Drafted into nature's poem,
he has outrun loneliness,
erased his human algorithm.
Leaving but a black seed,
sunk in the red clay,
by the maw of irrelevance.

Emotion's calculus intervenes.
Two women stop their car.
From nowhere, they summon
a man and his son. And
torn from sleep's shell,
assaulted by compassion,
old *Pantanero* is set back
on solitude's long straight road.

Bitter Taste

Backbone sprawled across the Milky Way,
vertebrae afloat among the constellations,
sleep shielded by altitude, warmed
by the south-face granite,
the volatile *pinyon* risen
from the balsamic throat
of the forest below
where frail, the stomping,
lithe, the shiver
in the cross-hairs of thrill
and fear that awaken you
to hunger and anticipation.
Excess of acuity pleats the spine.
Sharp eyes confound distance.

Pillowed gymnastics down the crag
to the fresh savor of meat, a first bite
in which prey overcomes predator.
A world tasted, spattered.
Abiding by animal rules, never vindictive....

Freedom – what an insult! –
gives you away. A hunting cacophony
attempts to humble you.
Supine summer night ends
with your fall to the hounds
and the filing away of bold innocence.

Puma Weather

In the lifted austral steppe, melodic
with upheaval, smeared with shadows,
humanity no longer knows itself.

Space made room for wind
to alight on the glaciers,
spraying a chill over the compass.

The blue-eyed puma, fit,
fittingly there, fitted
to weather and distances,

daily reinvents living things,
quickening to the heart beat of prey,
to their ways, alarm and glee.

The setting sun parades on the cat's
loose toying muscles,
before his next vanishing trick.

Mated with outer silence,
where his tail flails the stars,
he leaves not a trace of guilt.

A tributary runs, pollen drifts
past his penciled muzzle
stained a crimeless red,

when, warm from his kill,
he sets down to nap,
melting back into the dark

of the long sweeping night
of humble passion,
where none ever beg.

Stampede

In the dim cave where he sleeps,
ancient fingers dipped in clay,
spotted him long ago
as the clever one.

He sits on his haunches,
cameo carved out of dawn.

His back turned to everything,
but the dust billows painting
a fresco of running *wildebeest,*
he makes their lungs gasp
and their vertebrae stretch.

They pound past him,
solemn with dread,
bouncing off one another,
copious and clumsy,
rocking antelopes
herded by panic,

in a flood of sweat,
rising from earth's
stern game of survival.

He dresses subtly,
mottled with shadow and light,
trigger cocked, fire held,
coy killer,
graceful arsenal.

Sun brightens, shadow bundles,
boils over, turns vaporous,
begins the chase.

Something laughs in the mind,
aches at the sight of his acrobatics
and smooth execution, the fast gorging
that keeps us all going.

Night Fauna

In my sleep of jungle, steppe and sea
appears a favorite bestiary.

Darkness brings a leopard flung across a branch,
sleek with the slumber of ages,
pinning his markings on the sky.
I lay under the tent of his pelt,
hearing raucous rumbles.

Eyes half closed to the rhythmic
clench and stretch of a tiger's paws,
snow mittens, petals of fire,
fragrant with creamy marrow.
None can fight
this limpid splendor
so I nestle close
to his weapons.

Otter rockets through
fluid acumen,
absorbs lightening in
her wired coat.
Nimble otter,
how far shall we drift together?

Horse drums a canter,
exalting speed,
infinite dactylography.
Impetuously writes out
the algorithm of his odyssey.

At last, a great god confides in me.

Stalking a Dialogue

Woman: What are you there,
               dressed to kill,
                lording the spiky acacia,
                with the clock of your heart
                wound up so tight?

Leopard: A sunlit figment, a breath of sun,
                yet cooler than ice,
                fluid through night's twine,
                candor's last enactment,
                shrine of once upon a time.

Woman: Give me the yellow sapphire of your stare,
                allow me onto your hypnotic path,
                wake me to dawn's stretch on the tree limb.

Leopard: I fear the gangs in which
                the hero's hairless skin
                is bedecked with my demise.
                My hope lies in keeping
                what I can stalk.

Woman: You are a dotted line of suspense.
                Your stare sets the sun of
                knighthood's repose under a tree.

Leopard: I am not a pattern
                to allay your sideway longings.
                I am absence to every kill.

Woman: There you hang, priceless stole,
                paws dripping daylight,
                enacting transmutation between
                the thorns of time and space.

Leopard: The smell and weight of clouds,
the shivering branches
against a spinning sky,
the wet glut of flesh between
rough tongue and rutted bark…
What else can there be
beyond the instant's elixir?

Woman: Draw me a flat riled skull,
chiseled under the staring stars.
Yawn sharp canines at me. Catch me.

Leopard: To wonder at each other is the beginning of all peril.

Moon Fox

Summer nights become him.
Heavy-scented and lewd,
they come to him.

The moon blows a bubble
of chill fire and craft
over his Madame X profile.

He sits on the tarmac,
lean in the nose and legs,
a humble curve down his back,

content in his short-lived glory,
before some fool runs him over.
(Why can't people be more fox?)

Now he stares back,
bright and bold,
aglow from above.

The trees want him, the streams
rustle to quench his thirst.
Searching the head lights
with star dust eyes,

he runs off, exulting
with animal passion.

November, Four pm

Autumn tattooed a duck's eye.
The forest floor chiseled out a jewel.
Yellow ore runs underfoot.
Memory shuffled into foresight.

Unreason makes overtures to the brain.
Thrown by a nuclear deity, a gold disk
shines across evening's first yawn.
A falling leaf mummifies in mid-air,
crackles before death,
bottled in acrid coma.
Instantly, rebirth writes out
its green label.

In my head throbs bark's pulse.
High and low, the spokes of cycle spin
towards remedy. And though
the essence of all this still
eludes the prowling senses,
though lucidness fails to understand,
and the reader of this may not cry out:
"That's it!",
four pm's perfusion of gold
vamps up my blood and softens the riddle.

A Japanese Garden in a French Mind

Stylization intended for a wall tells none
where earth ends and heaven begins.

A flat landscape, in fact, so the eye
can make up any joyous prospect,

though the garden hides nothing
and revels in its integrity,

blinding me to any other,
terrestrial, or oftentimes invoked.

Here, a season of powdery mimosa,
emitting warmth in long-haired breezes

of imperial silk, of which the embroideries
wandered off beyond their hem

— blue nymphs, orange sea stars —
into a pearly extinction of darkness.

Unalloyed yellow from which gold was extracted,
left hanging on branches in a corner,

the gilt mood of divinity against a haze of faith
where bright flowers fragrantly orbit.

The blossomed air plays the eternal Spring,
pumping sun into my lungs.

The Capital

In Spring the stylish streets
lay numb with ecstasy
from days and nights
beside carnal gardens,
in which tall-windowed houses
stood stately behind their columns.

Under the sky funded by rooftops,
the city preened and
pulled on its moorings.

Out went my parents, fleet
with cold war jazz,
when dusk did its southern prance
and traffic played clarinet
across the river,
onto the swooning curbs
where street lamps blew them
mist and good wishes.

Mother's Florentine profile
hung rubies among the stars.
Father was never careful with his smiles.
Somehow, of all things out there,
I was the nerve and center.

PHANTOMS

Sissi's Villa

The empress promenades
during timeless interludes,
walking her pet starvations
on ballroom gown terraces,
mapped with boxwood alleys,
the lapidarian capture
of Olympians in sculpture. Still,
they hold out daggers of silence
to stab her at every step.
Stygian cypresses,
cryptic immortals,
pillar a villa dressed
in sunrise silks, phoenix fans
swished by the hand of a breeze.
Horizon of the scrolled Ionian sea
adulates her.

By late afternoon, troubled
by the rural peace below
that carries on living,
leaving her so alone,
she runs down the front steps,
raked shallow by light,
to posturing laurels and pine,
sowing her melancholy,
even as she flees
the blight of relentless fame.

Red Gloves in Umbria
(in memory of gloves seen in Bergamo and from reading Vernon Lee)

House in Umbria
on a November afternoon
scarred by an atrophied sun.

Neither castle nor farm,
but a pensive forehead framed
by gilded spirals of trance,

impervious to humdrum,
feeling with defiance
the ground shudder deep down.

By stucco and stone
the *Rocca* has settled
on the unstable font.

Rooms narrate frescos,
vaultings macerate old terrors.
Cornelian urns, ebony cabinets

from four centuries past,
fragile, mortuary,
seem short of breath.

Handstitched, these gloves.
Scarlet and fuchsia kid skin,
are minutely sewn together.

Never meant to be worn,
their bloom, unknown to botany,
flaunts its vain glory

on a console's careful polish.
There, the living reflect
the immortal likeness of themselves.

Defined by elegance,
with only itself for god,
none here practice time or theology.

Permanent dissent
orchestrates the senses
in a minor scale of exile.

Under the dank moon, a pool
like a goat's malevolent eye,
keeps out the countryside.

A tiered garden put up
hedges inside where the gloves
dress up statues as wraiths.

Wound up birds warble
elegies and fly across
the exsanguinous sun.

Through peristyles of fog
spreads a musky spell
from the wicked pair.

Transformation

I walk a corridor fashioned by a footstep,
beyond the elusive presence of one
I wish to catch up with.
Weightless feet over parabolic floors
of a vertiginous globe,
between rhetorical walls imprinted
with stark solitude,
roping in memory's fragments,
held by vestiges of gravity.

Who then walks this wadded ether?
Through the lacquer silence, still,
hums a mood of life.
In lavish rooms, so poised,
that I cannot help longing
to be someone I once knew.
Best are corners of intimacy,
guarding objects, as poignant
as the waning of a dear voice.
I contemplate a fire of remembrance
in a dragon's metal wings,
a coral dew on evening's sideboards,
an atoll puff from a cigarillo,
a greenhouse wrist tickled by a cuff,
a crusty smell of loaves conjured
by appetite's figment,
and the inhospitable truth
that I once lived here.

Outside, a flannel grey façade, kept
free from nature's snares, looks
on with a thousand yard stare.
A stream runs through sprockets of light,
flowing with cruel benevolence
and sweltering recollections
of summer relief,
deep dark river on puckered skin
in water's cool dialect.
Were I to share these walls
with the green attar of trees
and moss, I would feel once more
the breeze of favorite places,
gateways that men forfeit to live on.

Pisani Palace

I pass beneath your windows
because tall rather than wide,
they formulate promises
and invite to look up inside.
Octagonal panes of carbonated glass
transform sunlight
into a flagon's essence
of which, at every passage,
I feel the hermetic sweetness,
poisoned or perfumed.

Drop by drop, soundlessly fall
elusive sprites of dusk.
They bear standards of memory
inscribed with question marks
about aureate fantasies
in which answers hide
as in the heart's depths.

Pisani still stands above water,
contriving nightmare from dream.
Stony eyebrows convey me to rooms
that sneak from seduction to murder,
costumed in shrouds of history.
Each stalwart statue
proclaims the ascendancy of a ghost
and the inscrutable nature of a shadow.

The pages of its palatial life turn
back and forth with no sense of time,
to reach an apex of yearning,
the gate through which to enter.

Eyes penciled vague,
pale flames in my hair,
I walk the endless halls
followed by my skirt's rustle
ever crossing dismal thresholds.

Alter Ego

The boy and I enter early dawn's aspic of moisture and air,
as two units of being, scissored out of space,
tingling with death up and down our spines
in this disembodied capital of ghosts.
A tourmaline dome covers the river of miracles
that flows devouring whole tiers of urban filth,
but for memory's haze ascending the *ghats*
in blue cobras of smoke.
Between acrid intakes, the alternative of a stench.
Morning's prayers careen down the Ganges to Yon's frontline
in a contagion of candles and awe,
like ragamuffins going through a department store.
The boy and I, convinced to be more than ourselves.
He sees her first and his licorice hair falls
in disquiet over his canine eyes. He hates disloyalty.
Her resemblance to me is essential, pervasive:
from boat to boat we replicate each other.
Which part of the aberration am I?
On which side of the mirror?
Do I go where she goes?
Who dissolves the other into dream?
Already the sun strides up the river towards us
and something of passing time rouses nostalgia.
She pushes upstream with a staccato of oars in the locks,
while, with suspicious ease, I glide seaward.
Our two crafts pass each other.
One of us slips back into the crypt of absence,
invisibility's deletion.
Did the boy invent me? Only he can reassure me
that it was divine trickery
of the fanged goddess of death and rebirth.

The Last Morning

Nearly all is still offered by a vigilant kindness.
To see him pass, a bald tree patched with moss,
jumped over a brick wall
behind which dozes an orchard.
A bird roused by dawn melts the night frost.
A moment hovers in place, sovereign,
articulates memories from the headlines of his past.
Boldly, fresh air holds out a hand to him to run for it.
Even the billowing grey sky shapes a talisman
and his eyes gleam with forest escape.
Invisible peripheries signal their beauty.
The man prays for the jingle of a bit
in a horse's mouth,
for the rivered neck of equine strength.
No one knows anymore how to love
his flesh poised on the edge of abstraction.
He is the bottom of a well, already
his reflection effaced by a dripping toll.
Darkness clangs shut, silence knots with steel.
Horror is a solo performance.
He parts from his distant scream.
The smoking pyre has nothing to show for it.

On the Moon

Sleepless hologram   of the moon
platinized erring
after a landing manufactured
by childish delectation   according to the beginning
of a comic strip adventure   imbued with Hergé optimism
a nocturnal solo
voicing introverted light   on a hushed planet
under the lantern fest   of Hesperian starlight
my leaps abide by the genius of space
everywhere nothing other than isolation
from stunned dust bowls   to scabbed crests
haunted by galactic pull
in the highest octaves of indifference
that suddenly reverse the spell
and neighborhood stars lock their doors
and I mutate from explorer to intruder
renegade of bald rifts and craters   cold-pressed with oddity
the delusion of golden apple trees   arranged in staggered rows
sweating phantom juices   mourning alter ego shadows

a place of bereavement

of squamous solitude   shedding endless vistas
which had to dream escape   from prison turrets

desperation of being left behind

and then to look back   stung by freak nostalgia
of someone missed in that homeless ruin
of something not detected on time

Hunedoara

The castle holds its own against time.
Rebellious still, stomping the rock-bed it anchored to.

Some contract held darkly in the Gabbro window panes
Conserves unreality within

Even as summer outside blouses
Innocuously with pollens and breeze.

An albino approaches under a darkening sky
On the drawbridge, as if I were expected.

Chalk-faced child, uncertainly gendered,
A mist of features freckled with far constellations,

Who shrouds my crossing with something
Of a final departure.

The milk blue stare spilled from a mountain lake.
In the half-smile, sediments of devotion and malice,

A tense postponing of cruelty
As the albino comes closer.

Once the gate is passed,
A besieging of anomalies.

What seemed lost in time's funnel,
Spirals on endlessly.

Memories never owned
Burst through riddled masonry.

A courtyard sharpens with anger,
Steel sparring in the corners.

A gutted tower re-inhabits itself
With fireplace flickers on fur and tapestry.

Residents crowd me, suggest
That they have long known me.

In Knights Hall the colonnade digs down
To the roots of human hell,

Inevitably propagating
From remains of suffering below.

In these hollows of abandon
A violence will not let me go.

A Case for Reincarnation

Today my life will hit remote and repeat
to reformulate you according to a flux of scenery,
relying on nature's sibylline messages that
necessarily have become our go-betweens.

Through dark cloaked trees toward east and west,
over moss runners where boulders ruminate.
Of course, I suspected your existence
before that precarious meeting.

Its you I see gazing at a river
in the hard-edged style of a Strelnikov,
contemplating the wherewithal of regeneration,
risking to forego your true self,
and all fancy beneath your skull
on which hair grows with a hint of flames
– as if I had not noticed the causal fire.

Around you, the whisper of one missed
fills your silence with reticence.

But the knight must have hardship,
each heartbeat devoted to duty.
At times, no doubt, you are shaken,
unruliness lifts you to the zing of stars,
above the busy road of equality.
Mountains, woods, rivers absorb
your inner derelictions, distill them
back into your blood as remedy.

One day, when you are gone,
I will see the hue of your presence
in the basking of an autumn sun,
seeking me out with arms of light.
For you and I were ever before,
as now and to be.
With nothing but inklings,
no common address,
yet our certainty remains.

Chemistry

There arises in the room an initial warning
within unexpected molecules of plenitude.
What is this, in fact? Certainly off the normal track.
Too much to be a moment forgotten in times ahead.
The nameless procedures of the day plod on
same as ever.
The dust pale leaves of summer pretend
to tiptoe across the office walls.
The heat outside contradicts the winter
of the grey uniform paint
scratched and nicked with campaign defeats.
A rag of sun wipes away
this Tolstoy winter of ice and snow.
A fly buzzes over the warped sill
– piled and complicated with papers,
with other life signatures clamoring their due –
with hysterical wings, fans a delirium.

Our skin is fired with erythrism,
buttons leave flesh untold.
Our lips aspire to the nude punctuation of love,
Our bodies incline, then sidle to keep away,
shy away from confrontation.
A shadow-boxing of wish and refusal
on either side of the desk.

The room fills to the brim with our wilderness
of birch, stream, clanship and telepathic breezes.
Pity makes its passionate plea,
gives an ultimate caress
against the final blight of death.

Light Stepping

Beyond straining senses
stillness, inexplicably,
absorbs tremors of feather, hair, scale and leaf.
Even though I crack a twig underfoot,
side-stepping silence willfully,
I am numbed by its touch.
Platinum webs across dawn's re-facing,
spring their explicit charts upon the mind,
and lofty above dew banks,
immortal spiders at the center of their Thangka.
Trees hang inarticulate memory upon the mist
in togas and orchid-trimmed robes.
Things drink, bloom, expel, stretch above
debris, to stem to bark to creature
to vigor to death to resurrection
of all parts reshuffled.
In exuberant Pleiades, birds among the leafage,
flowers high nesting,
replications of liana and python,
a cat's jasmine trace caught in the grass
where musky herds step warily.
Movement pocked with sun and shadow.
A paw swift with murder,
matted the ground with gore and skin,
and as you crouch to measure a print,
the quiet no longer is of tigers and leopards evading,
but yours, resolute, feverish hush
battling my approximate reason.
Kingdom unto yourself,
sharp lifting gaze, eyes of a Mongol storm.
Brave, handsome smile, gentle
boldness free of claims of wisdom.
Wild with despondency and joy,
custodian of the jungle.

Himalayan Foothills

The Great Hornbill wades through the air,
flapping like a wet sheet
from branch to branch
over the Ramganga gush
of agate, jade, aquamarine.
Our backs to Vedic boulders,
we search a perspiring forest,
past the quick blossoming
of red bauble birds,
the blue lightening of a Kingfisher,
a Yellow Bittern's flitting,
never to revisit that day,
inducing us to hide on a ledge
under cover of some trees.
Already, a sense of peril fills our former spot.
Beyond the beach's curve,
we pray the tiger will not hear us,
but will come to drink,
maw slack, eyes blinking
gently in self-radiance,
picking out the sand trail between the stones,
plying armored paws over our tracks.
The trees slightly quiver,
granite rocks harden their starkness.
We wait to no avail.
But returning to camp, we see
his scrapes across our footprints.

What Snuck up on Them

These lovers played at madness
obligated to their kind of youth.

Was it not so then?

On that brazen austral land
the couple followed the scent of impulse
through the sweet and sour gardens that
honed what still held on to barbarisms.

They steered for blossom downpours,
sun-sparkled lawns.
The Southern Cross spread over them
its galactic gossamer of runes.

Until midday they spun
wheels of good fortune
around hoary, contemplative trees.

At noon they took refuge
in the solemn shade
of a bamboo grove
that hushed them.

In pachyderm quiet
poles yawned and screeched.
A hint of gloom
crawled among the greens.

On the papered ground
fallen tusks began to grow
between his feet, multi-limbed
enigmas, hybrids of underworld,

and though she ushered him away,
his eyes had now forgotten her,
his clothes moved without him,

his silence filled with imprecations.
His arms flailed against nothing seen,
horrors that excluded her.

By the livid light of madness,
they were dispossessed
of their island.

In the Silence After the Bird's Call

Mountainous island on an intemperate sea,
in a tapestry of fog
hollowed by silence.
Enchantment,
kept in a safe.

Secrecy hides the code,
prudence wears a mask,
mist fills my eyes.
Yet, how not to see
disguise in this torpor?

Inland from ocean's recitations,
just after the Barbet's overture
to my wishes by a pond
as quiet as a dormitory,
I wonder: 'is it so?'

Wading through intuition,
I suspect somewhere
a rainbow of pelts.
Rafts of vapor lift me
to hyphened parapets of insight.

Drawing clouds on itself,
nature conceived a youth
mischievous and coy.
Over there, a careening
in the branches,
a long tail act
by a mottled gymnast.
'You're still here,' sighs relief.

A Kind of Anniversary

This morning before hours lined up
we were nearly together again
in a rubellite dawn above a rosemary sea.
Winged by an absence of time
I was beyond myself
and because of distance
I knew the closeness between us.
Your place and mine superimposed,
interchanged, convinced
of this eventuality,
a faraway dragon shimmer.
The paddling of the breeze
through summer's silk
felt like arms and lips. Yours.
The clearings of my eyes filled
with swift rivers, swiping bears
blushing fish. I inhaled
the apothecary birch woods
the crushed fern of your skin.
Today was a celebration
of our past defeat, of
the barren smiles of confusion
and delinquent silence.
Across steppes, lakes, mountains
we were in each other's hunger,
enamored through recall.

Paradise Predicted

A pale sun on a watery pane in Jermyn street,
the real sun is the knotted yellow tie.
Pipe smoke drifting through the fog,
a tree losing brown leaves to a lawn
where you walk in the finest tan shoes.

A cat draws stripes over a *petit point* cushion,
one narrowed eye on his keepers
toasting the snow,
the other on the garden,
white with Christmas.

Concrete tenements softened
to poetic melancholy
by the proximity of a house
where a great writer wrote his best.
Next block, bare branches extend
to a rotund and ornate theater
with the linear obsession of desire.

Head in the clouds
of a cloudless sky,
an island promises other islands
fashioned from the rack and pinion
of heavenward thought,
where lacy insects play strings,
laundered sand beats water's pulse,
sirens swim the night, long-limbed,
through inter-planetary currents,
gods wear their hair loose.
Blissful anatomies, astounding profiles.

You are some thousand miles away.
The old city quivers,
laps and wheezes with cold,
reasserting its mystery
in red pigments and batrachian plops
beneath the hanging lanterns,
pendants of the night.
Just as my heart might shatter
you're as near as a whisper
bridge after bridge.

www.ingramcontent.com/pod-product-compliance
Lightning Source LLC
Chambersburg PA
CBHW022117090426
42743CB00008B/892